WHISPERED MELODIES

SEBEEDHA

Made with ❤ on the Notion Press Platform

www.notionpress.com

Contents

Preface

Whispered melodies is a collection of my personal reflections and musings on life, love, loss, and everything in between. Each poem and short story is a piece of my heart, a snapshot of a moment in time, and a testament to the human experience. As a writer, I believe that words have the power to heal, to inspire, and to connect us with one another. My hope is that this collection will do just that - touch your heart, uplift your spirit, and bring you a sense of connection to the world around you.

In Whispered Melodies, you will find a range of emotions - from the raw and painful to the joyful and hopeful. Each poem and story is a reflection of my own experiences, and I hope that by sharing them with you, you will feel less alone in your own journey. It is my sincere hope that this book will bring you comfort, inspiration, and a renewed appreciation for the beauty of life. Thank you for joining me on this journey, and I hope that these words will stay with you long after you have finished reading them.

Acknowledgments

I am thrilled to present Whispered Melodies, my first book, to the world. This collection of poems and short stories has been a labor of love, and I couldn't have done it without the support and encouragement of so many people.

First and foremost, I would like to thank my family and friends for their unwavering support and belief in me. Your love and encouragement have been a constant source of inspiration, and I am grateful for every moment we have shared together. I also want to express my gratitude to my publisher, who believed in my work and gave me the opportunity to share it with a wider audience.

To my readers, I thank you from the bottom of my heart. Your interest in my work and your willingness to give it a chance mean more to me than words can express. I hope that this book will touch your heart and inspire you to see the beauty in the world around you.

Finally, I want to acknowledge the many writers, poets, and storytellers who have inspired me along the way. Your work has enriched my life in countless ways, and I am grateful for the gift of your words.

Thank you all for being a part of this journey with me. I am excited to see where it takes us next.

Star Dust

Her bare foot paddled the damp soil.

The air was filled with petrichor,

It percolated to every crevice of her body

Awaking the pluviophile in her.

He was like the rain that, lingers luscious petrichor

When dripping in to the parched soil.

He stood behind her gently caressed her hair and,

Brushed it away from her soft cheeks.

His fingers traced her jawlines and,

He kissed her on her cheeks

Chilling her skin like the cool gentle breeze.

She turned around, her eyes shined like stars,

Face glowed like moon, drizzling

Raindrops sparkled on her hair like the cosmos.

She was the finest stardust that,

Quenched his astrophilic thirst

Nepenthe...

This irenic serein

Makes me serene,

Like an apricity in my

Melancholy.

Elysian abendrot

Which pulls me into an ambedo

Is my nepenthe.

I pretended not...

When you came closer to me

My heart beat fast

But I pretended not.

When you smiled at me

It was my euphoria

But I pretended not.

When you looked at me.

I wanted to gaze at you as I do

At the stars.

But I pretended not.

When you gave me roses and a ring

I wanted to say 'yes'.

But I pretended not.

When you loved me

I loved you back

But I pretended not

The Rain...

The rain taps her roof,

In tune with her melancholy,

Each drop a reminder,

Of the tears she cannot shed,

As depression's weight holds her steady.

Cross Roads....

It was a cold evening. She was walking alone through the woods, through the orange- red muddy road. The trees were covered with mosses and ferns, fog and mist weaved a white blanket and the whole place was immersed in silence, pin drop silence. The silence did not cause any fear in her, she did not even feel the biting cold. Everything was still and serene. Only she was moving, it was the throb of her heart that broke the silence. It was slower much slower than ever.

She started to move faster and faster, she came across the cross-roads. She stopped there for a moment, her life stretched out before her. Her life was always like standing across the cross-roads. The left road was muddy and lonely which lead to dreams, fulfillments, self-love and self-respect, she always took right one which was muddy and grassy.

She has always lived for others. She has spent her whole life fulfilling their dreams and finding solutions to their problems. To this day, she has lived in fear of hurting others with her actions and words. She whelved all her dreams and desires to fulfil the expectations of those around her. She cast aside her favorite clothes and food for others. Despite her intense desire to fall in love and be loved, she did not. She turned down all the love requests that came before her. She buried all the love that had bloomed in her heart. She taught herself that she could never love anyone, to save someone's pride. She lived her every day for others, believing that was her happiness.

She did not realize that she was not living her life but that it belonged to others. For whom she gave up everything, none of them is with her today. Those with whom she spent her time don't have a single moment to spend with her. Today, she is a failure for them, a misfortune.

She started walking again, but this time she took the left one, which was lonely. She continued to walk further. She slowed down as she reached her destination, the one and only decision she had ever taken for her. She slowly walked to the edge of the cliff closed her eyes, and then jumped down. She built her wings on the way down.

Charcoal....

In blackened wood, we find our light,
Charcoal, a treasure that's always in sight.
A reminder that from ashes we rise,
With the help of the flames that burn so wise.

The spark ignites, the flames take hold,
Charcoal's story begins to unfold.
From glowing embers, it builds a fire,
A source of warmth, a burning desire.

The smell of smoke, the crackling sound,
Charcoal's magic is all around.
It cooks the food, it warms the soul,
It's the essence of heat, a powerful goal.

A symbol of strength, a force of might,

Charcoal burns with an inner light.

Its darkness hides a secret power,

A primal energy that we devour.

Charcoal, a mystery, a work of art,

A creation born from nature's heart.

It speaks of transformation, of change so deep,

A reminder to us all, to never sleep.

For like charcoal, we too can change,

Transformed by the fires that we arrange.

With each new day, a chance to ignite,

And burn with a power that shines so bright.

It grills the meat, it roasts the corn,

Charcoal flames are born to adorn.

The smell that wafts from a burning pile,

Is a memory that lasts for miles.

Charcoal, the tool of the artist's trade,

It brings to life the images they've made.
The soft, black lines that dance across the page,
Creating depth and beauty, a timeless sage.

Charcoal on paper, a dance so wild,
Lines and curves, like a playful child.
The blackness of charcoal, so raw and bold,
Creates a painting, a story to be told.

The artist's hand moves swiftly, with grace,
A symphony of lines, taking its place.
A portrait emerges, from the depths of dark,
A masterpiece of art, a fiery spark.

The charcoal painting, a story to tell,
Of human lives, of beauty and hell.
It captures the essence of our world,
A window into a life, unfurled.

With each stroke of the charcoal stick,

A masterpiece takes form, brick by brick.

Shadows and light, a world in between,

A charcoal painting, a vision so keen.

Charcoal, the medium so raw and real,

It captures our hearts, it makes us feel.

The power of art, to move and inspire,

Is like the heat of charcoal's burning fire.

For in the blackness of charcoal's mark,

We find a light that's glowing, like a spark.

A reminder of life's beauty and its pain,

And the power of art, to forever remain.

Ash....

Ash, the remnants of what once was,
A symbol of endings and inevitable loss,
Of fire and smoke, of destruction and decay,
Of the passing of time, of things that don't stay.

Ash reminds us of the fragility of life,
Of how everything we hold dear will one day die,
Of the ephemeral nature of all we see,
And the importance of cherishing each memory.

For though ash may be the end of one thing,
It's also the start of what the next may bring,
A blank slate for the future to be made,
A reminder that even in endings, there's a way to pave.
In the quiet aftermath of fire,
The ash remains, a solemn choir,

Whispering of what once was there,

Before it all turned to smoke and air.

But though the flames may have destroyed,

The ash is proof that life's enjoyed,

For what once stood so tall and grand,

Has left behind this humble brand.

And in the midst of all this grey,

A new beginning hides away,

For from these ashes can arise,

A spark of hope that never dies.

So let the ash settle on the ground

Let it lay where it has been found

For from its darkness, light will grow

And from its pain, new hope will flow

Summer....

Now it's summer, and the

Sun shines bright

Clear blue sky and chirping birds

The air is fruity

The bees are boozy

My bare feet kiss the lush green

And I feel serene

The wind plays with my hair

Summer is in the air.

Let It Go...

She was insulted

She was abandoned

She was stabbed

She was hurt

She was wounded

She was bled

She was broken

She was shattered

She was withered

But she healed

Cause she let it go.

The humming bird....

She was in her off white night gown. She was reclining on a deck chair in veranda watching a humming bird building its nest in the rose wines that climbed on to the roof. She has been watching it for the past week. A few years before, there was a hibiscus hedge around the garden. The flowers were dark red in color with five fragile petals. Every morning there used to be a bouquet of humming birds feeding on the flower nectar.

As she continued to watch the hummingbird, she couldn't help but notice its intricate movements. The tiny bird would dart back and forth, carrying bits of twigs and leaves in its beak, carefully weaving them together to create a cosy little nest. It was a mesmerizing sight, and she found herself spending hours watching the bird at work.

Over the course of the week, she had seen the hummingbird make incredible progress on its nest. It was now a small, circular structure, perched high up in the rose vines. She marvelled at the bird's dedication and hard work, even as she wondered how it managed to fly back and forth so effortlessly, carrying materials that were often twice its size.

As she sat on the veranda, she couldn't help but think about the hibiscus hedge that used to be in the garden. It had been one of the main attractions of the house, and she had spent countless hours admiring the bright red flowers and the hummingbirds that visited them. It had been heart breaking when the hedge had to be removed, but she was comforted by the sight of the hummingbird building its nest.

She remembered the day the hedge was removed, and how she had spent the afternoon sitting on the veranda, watching as the workers uprooted the plants one by one. The hummingbirds had been visibly upset, darting around frantically, unsure of what was happening to their favourite feeding spot. It had been a sad day, but now, as she watched the hummingbird at work, she felt a sense of renewal.

She wondered if the hummingbird knew how much joy it was bringing to her life. As if sensing her thoughts, the tiny bird flew over to the veranda and perched on the railing, chirping softly. She couldn't help but smile, feeling a sense of connection with the creature.

As the days passed, the hummingbird's nest grew bigger and more elaborate. It was now a complex structure, with multiple layers of twigs and leaves woven together to create a sturdy and comfortable home for the bird's upcoming brood. She knew that it wouldn't be long before the eggs were laid, and she looked forward to watching the baby hummingbirds grow and learn to fly.

In the evenings, she would sit on the veranda with a cup of tea, watching as the hummingbird flitted around the nest, tending to her eggs. It was a peaceful and calming ritual, and she felt grateful for the little bird's presence in her life.

As the summer days turned into fall, the hummingbird's nest became quieter, and she knew that the birds had flown away to start their own lives. But she would always cherish the memories of watching the tiny bird at work, building her nest and raising her young. It was a reminder of the resilience and beauty of nature, and the importance of taking time to appreciate the small wonders.

Unspoken Words....

His lips parched, no words would come,

Though he struggled to speak with all his might.

His tongue cleaved to the roof of his mouth,

The secret he wished to impart remains unknown,

Lost forever with his final breath and departing groan

No words escaped, despite his effort and defiance,

He gasped for breath, then succumbed to the eternal drought.

His unspoken thoughts, forever sealed.

Sweet Sour Memory....

Under the tamarind tree we would play,

With laughter and joy we'd start our day,

The sun would rise, the sky so blue,

And there we'd be, me and my cousin too.

We'd search for tamarind, scattered on the ground,

Their sweet and sour taste, so easily found,

And with a scarf, we'd make a bag,

Collecting the fallen fruits, like a treasure we'd snag.

One morning, our bag was full to the brim,

Our efforts had paid off, our faces aglow and dim,

We looked at each other, so proud and content,

Our little adventure, the best time ever spent.

With each tamarind, memories we'd make,

Our bond as cousins, forever it'll take,

Under the tamarind tree, we'll always meet,

With each fallen fruit, our bond we'll greet.

Orange tree....

In the heat of summer, she felt so hungry,

So she climbed up a tree, feeling rather plucky,

She plucked oranges from the branches up high,

And ate them with relish, under the bright sky.

Her belly was full, her eyes grew heavy,

The branches cradled her, safe and steady,

But soon she was asleep, lost in dreams,

And didn't notice the tree's warning screams.

With a snap and a crack, the branch gave way,

And our sleepy heroine fell down in dismay,

But instead of landing hard on the ground,

The oranges cushioned her, safe and sound.

She woke up with a start, feeling rather silly,

To find herself lying on a bed of fruit so juicy and chilly,

She laughed and giggled, feeling quite merry,

And ate more oranges, until she was nearly.

Bougainvillea……

Summer's vibrant hue

A burst of colors

Natures painted brush

Thorny branches sprawl and climb,

With leaves that flutter in the wind and chime,

Bougainvillea blooms bright pink.

Withered Rose....

A withered rose lies,

Fragrance gone, petals wilted,

Fading beauty mourns,

Withered petals, once so lush,

Time's fleeting embrace.

Rose....

When I was a flower bud in my childhood

I longed to be kissed by the sun, hoping to blossom into a flower.

During my adolescence,

When I began to blossom into a flower,

I got thrilled by dreaming, butterflies and bees swarming around me.

When I reached my youth

When everyone was mesmerized by my beauty,

When butterflies sucked honey from me, I was well proud.

I was proud not to remember that the length of my life was only a few days.

If once I wished to be kissed by the sun,

Today I want to run away from him

Now I can see the signs of ageing in my petals.

The signs became clearer and clearer as he kissed me every day

Hey butterflies and bees, please come back to me

Of course, I'm old now and

Indeed, I don't have anything sweet other

Than memories but come to me once more,

Before I fall..........................

Phoenix.....

She is a warrior

Who fought it all alone

Marks on her wrist

Counts the war she fought.

She is the gold

That once was buried deep

Then molten in the burning furnace

Graven and hammered.

She is a Phoenix

Who burned herself in her past

And reborn from the ashes of

Her past.

Them.....

Along the long road with trees of yellow hue,

A girl with a ponytail walks with her beau.

Expressive eyes and beauty so true,

Her mole adds charm to her face that glows.

The boy, tall and thin, with innocence in his eyes,

A smile on his face and black hair so fine,

He rides his cycle slowly, by her side,

As they both share laughter, joy and time.

The girl, tall and slim, with hair of black,

Her ponytail swings with every step she takes,

A sight so sweet that one can't keep track,

Of how much their love for each other makes.

The trees and flowers, a sight so serene,

A perfect setting for love to be seen,

As they walk and ride, with hearts so keen,

Their love, a story forever to be gleaned.

The long road, a witness to their love,

A tale of two hearts that fit like a glove,

The girl with her ponytail and her love,

Together, they walk on the path they behoove

As they walk, the world fades away,

Their love is all that they have today.

In this moment, nothing else matters,

Their love is all that flatters.

The long road ahead, they will travel,

Together, with love that will never unravel.

She....

She walks on the shore

Her eyes blue as the sea

Her hair like the waves

Her skin like the pearl

Her smile like the spoon drift

She holds secrets deep as the Ocean.

Wild Daisies....

As wild daisies, we stood tall and proud in our meadow, basking in the warm sun and gentle breeze. We have witnessed many things in our meadow, but the day we witnessed a murder was one we will never forget. We stood tall, swaying gently in the breeze, as a car drove onto the lush grass of our home, carrying with it three people whose fates were intertwined. The first man was tall and clean-shaven, with a look of frustration etched on his face. The woman was a striking figure with tanned skin, curly hair, and a sharp jawline, but her expression was one of sadness and gloom. The second man was muscular, with tanned skin and hazel eyes that gleamed in the sunlight.

As we looked on, we could sense the tension between them growing. They argued fiercely, and we could feel the anger and resentment radiating off of them. Suddenly, the woman drew a gun and shot the second man. His blood spilled out onto the grass and our white petals, staining us crimson, the evidence of his violent end. The first man was frightened and confused, and we could sense his panic as he realized what had just happened. The two of them carried the dead body and placed it in the car before speeding away. We witnessed everything, but no one asked us. We stood in silent vigil, watching as the world around us continued on its endless march. But we will always remember the day that violence came to our peaceful meadow, and we will always bear witness to the secrets hidden within our petals.

Two Souls....

Two hearts intertwine,

Entwined in passion

Two souls lost in each other,

Soft whispers in the moonlight,

Love's sweet symphony.

Unopened Book....

With pages yet to turn and tales
Untold, like an unopened book,
He stood before me, a mystery to behold.
His secrets locked up, his stories unknown,

But I was drawn to the enigma that he was,
His captivating presence, his every move a quiz.
I longed to delve into his depths and see
All that lied beyond the surface mystery.

So I took a chance, and opened the book,
Explored the depths, with every look.
For within those pages, I found a treasure,
His story unfolded, revealing its grace
A life of experiences, beyond measure.

The Guitarist….

With nimble fingers and a soulful heart,

He strums his guitar and makes it art.

The music flows like a gentle stream,

A soothing balm, a waking dream.

With strings as his wand, he weaves his spell

Creating beauty that words cannot tell

Each chord a wonder, sweet and grand

His music, a balm for the soul's demand.

Mary had a little lamb, he plays

in a way that leaves us all in daze.

The handsome guitarist, captivating and grand

His black hair falls over his forehead so fine,

And his black eyes, windows to his soul

His love of music, making us feel whole.

The notes rise and fall like waves,

And the crowd is hushed, enchanted and brave.

They listen with reverence and awe,

As he pours his heart out, without a flaw.

He plays with fire, he plays with grace,

And every note paints a different face.

The guitar is his voice, his muse,

A symphony of joy and blues.

The girl in the mountains....

Through misty mountains, she wanders free,

Her heart alive with curiosity.

With each step, she climbs higher still,

Breathing in the cool, crisp mountain chill.

She walks alone, but not alone,

For nature's spirits guide her home.

The trees and streams, the rocks and hills,

All whisper secrets that only she feels.

The trees stand tall, their branches spread,

And in their shade, she finds her bed.

The world around her is hushed and still,

As she wanders on with an unbreakable will.

With nimble feet, she climbs the hills,

Through valleys deep and trickling rills.

The mist surrounds her like a cloak,

As she wanders on with hope and hope.

With every step, she finds her way,

Discovering new paths with each passing day.

The misty mountains are her home,

And in their embrace, she'll never roam.

And as she walks, the mist begins to clear,

Her path ahead, now shining bright and clear.

With each step forward, she's stronger, bolder.

Cake....

He always loved to take long walks in the garden. He would spend hours strolling through the rows of blooming flowers and the tall trees that provided a canopy of shade. One day, as he was strolling through the garden's sprawl he noticed how the sun was high and the sky was a perfect blue. As he passed by the strawberries, he couldn't help, red and ripe, succulent and sweet. He picked them with care and delight. He popped one of them in to his mouth and had a burst of tangy goodness in his mouth. With apron on and sleeves rolled up, he entered the kitchen with a cup of sugar and flour, butter and eggs, to bake a cake. Mixing flour, sugar, and butter with care, he added eggs and milk to the mix, as he blended it, he felt a sense of bliss. He stirred the batter with flair. The batter was smooth and free of lumps, the aroma of vanilla filled the air. He sliced the strawberries with delicate care. The scent of strawberries filled the room. He poured the batter over the fruit so fresh, he smoothed the top with a gentle caress. He slid the cake in the oven with care.

He waited patiently, watching the clock's hand. When the cake was done, he sliced a piece, so soft and sweet, and savored every bite, so divine and neat. He closed his eyes and took a breath, the aroma wafting through his chest. A symphony of taste begun and the flavors danced upon his tongue. The moistness of the cake filled his heart with pure delight. He took another bite, a flavor so pure and bright, a moment that he'll never break, and a slice of heaven, so divine.

Hazel Eyes....

Those hazel eyes, a sight I'll never tire,

For they fill my heart with an eternal fire.

A pair of hazel eyes that greet me each day,

A sight to behold, so lovely and rare,

Oh, how I long to hold them, gaze into their depths,

To explore the secrets hidden within,

Burning Fire.....

Before the burning fire, she stood

Longing to leap in and become the smoke,

Soaring to the sky

To be the ash, merging with the soil

Or charcoal transformed into a masterpiece on canvas

Desert....

She was like the desert dry and bare

Yet full of life

Endless beauty in her soul

A mirage of hope

Dew Drops....

Silent morning mist,

Sparkling dew on blades of grass,

Nature's work of art.

Dew drops on petals,

A moment of pure beauty.

Spying Eyes.....

She walks through the crowd, unnoticed and unseen,

With a keen eye, sharp wit, and a mind that's keen,

She observes every detail, every move, and every sound,

For this girl is cunning, and her intelligence knows no bound.

With her spectacles perched on her nose, and her hair so long,

She's like a spy, stealthy and strong,

She listens, she watches, and she takes it all in,

For she has a talent to unravel secrets, a skill that's within.

She never shares what she knows, for her secrets are hers to keep,

But she uses her power, to climb high and leap,

For she's smart, she's clever, and she's always one step ahead,

A girl with a vision, a girl who's never misled.

Though she's short in stature, her mind is tall,

And her talents are unique, she's one of a kind, after all,

For she sees what others miss, and she hears what others don't,

And with her intelligence, she charts a path that's bold and upfront.

So if you see her, with her spectacles and her open hair,

Remember that she's more than meets the eye, and beware,

For this girl is cunning, observing, and intelligent too,

And with her special talent, there's nothing she can't do.

The house.....

A house with red roofs and white walls waiting for someone.

In the garden, where the grasses grow wild,

The lawns overgrown with weeds,

The breeze flirts with the wild daisies and carries

The faint aroma of the withered roses.

A house with red roofs and white walls waiting for someone.

Turquoise doors and windows waiting to be opened

To relieve the suffocating pain lingering inside.

Faded and cracked windows whisper about someone.

The whole house is immersed in silence.

Memories lurk in every corner, reflecting on the panes

To anguish someone in future.

A house with red roofs and white walls waiting for someone.

The rose vines laden with withered flowers

Crawled onto the roof.

Bees roam around the withered roses without

Quenching their thirst and are fatly baffled in the sun.

Ripened berries and juicy apples

Not gorged by the birds, got perished in the soil.

A house with red roofs and white walls waiting for someone.

Tarnished Christmas lanterns on the cracked wall and

The frayed rope swing tell the story

Of an evanescent halcyon.

Will the master come? To free it from its long haul

Imponderable!

Memories....

The scent of wax apples, guavas, and mangoes,
Takes me back to my childhood's sweet repose,
Where red hibiscus bloomed with grace,
And hummingbirds swayed at tranquil pace
How I yearn to retrace those memories once more,
And relive those moments of innocence and solace.

Ardour....

In the valley of Echor

Where the wild daisies grow

Where the calming river flows

She wandered in search of him.

He was her abiditory.

She ran to the river where

She first met him playing his violin.

He looked at her

She looked ravishing in her sapphire gown and

loose hair.

She sat beside him

Fireflies swarmed around them.

He removed the withered rose from her hair

And stroked her hair like playing a serenade on his violin.

He took her face in his arms letting her feel his Ardour

Her eyes sparkled making his face radiant.

She kissed him and

They slowly drowned in each other's soul.

Alive….

Her face pale like the fading moon

Her sunken eyes, windows of her soul

Reflects suffering and sorrow

Her lips wrinkled and dried

Her cheeks swollen and soaked in tears

Her body was still alive but, she was long dead

Marks on her wrist, even the death

Was not kind to her

Leaving her alive...........

Tunnel.....

"There is always light at the end of the tunnel"

They say, but I have not seen it yet.

"Keep running; you will reach the end" they

Say, but I haven't reached there yet.

"Be optimistic" they say, but I can't.

Once my eyes gleamed by a ray of light, I ran

To it hoping it to be the end

But, it was a freight train by which I was hit,

Bruised and bled.

"The light at the end is brighter than the dark

inside," they say, so I keep running and

Running but the tunnel goes on forever and

Ever......

Printed by Libri Plureos GmbH in Hamburg,
Germany